Brockhampton Estate

HEREFORDSHIRE

A souvenir guide

![The National Trust logo] THE NATIONAL TRUST

PARADISE ON EARTH

The Paradise Brook, which runs just to the north of Lower Brockhampton House, gives its name to the place: Brockhampton means 'the farm of the dwellers by the brook'. The name could hardly be more apt, as Brockhampton unites farms, people and landscape in tranquil harmony.

Farming through the ages

The Brockhampton estate comprises 680 hectares (1680 acres) of gently rolling woodland, fields and open parkland. The wooded slopes are cut by little valley streams (or 'dingles') with steep banks. The trees that grow in these secret places are the descendants of ancient woodland that has changed little over the centuries, as the rugged terrain makes it difficult to extract timber.

Brockhampton has been in continuous cultivation for over a thousand years, and the remains of the medieval ridge-and-furrow ploughing regime are still visible in some places.

The dense pattern of fields and hedges recorded on the 1737 estate map was simplified when the park was laid out in the 1760s, but the landscape has been altered surprisingly little since then. There is also a large percentage of unimproved permanent grassland, especially on Old Lincester Farm. Equally special are Brockhampton's orchards and hedgerows of damsons and other fruit trees, which support a wealth of mistletoe and wildlife.

A medieval manorial estate

The Brockhampton estate has been passed down in unbroken succession since the Middle Ages. At its historic heart is the late 14th-century Lower Brockhampton House with a picturesquely half-timbered little gatehouse and moat that have come to symbolise old Herefordshire. Many of the farmhouses and barns on the estate are almost as ancient, and continue to be used for the purpose for which they were intended, in accordance with the wishes of the donor, Colonel John Talbot Lutley. Brockhampton remains a working estate, but a beautiful one as well, with stunning views north and east to the Clee Hills, south and east to the Malverns and the Brecon Beacons.

Looking after Brockhampton

The National Trust is working to ensure that the chain is not broken, encouraging its five tenant farmers to farm their land in a sympathetic way that not only maintains the historic integrity and beauty of the estate, but also provides them with a decent income and a sustainable future.

Above Exploring Brockhampton

Opposite The Brockhampton estate is a mixture of arable, permanent pasture and woodland with superb views over the wider landscape

The most beautiful place in England

'One June evening of 1947 after a storm I walked down to Lower Brockhampton at dusk. The trees were dead quiet, not even whispering, and the undergrowth was steaming. A horizontal sunbeam from the west left the gatehouse in shadow. A middle-aged couple, whom I had not seen before, were leaning against the top gate. They were not speaking. "A lovely evening!" I said fatuously. "Yes," they replied. They were still there when I returned. I asked them if they came often. They explained that they lived in Bradford, Yorkshire, and visited Brockhampton twice a year. With the Colonel's consent they had scattered the ashes of their son in the park. He had been a pilot in the RAF. "After all," they said with conviction, "this must be the most beautiful place in England."'

James Lees-Milne

A HISTORIC ESTATE

There has been a settlement at Brockhampton since at least the time of the Domesday Book (1086). The place gave its name to its first owners, the Brockhampton family, who built the now-ruined Norman chapel. The estate then passed to the Domultons, who were responsible for constructing Lower Brockhampton House around 1380–1400 from giant timbers grown on the estate. During the first half of the 16th century, it was owned by the Habingtons. In 1552 Mary Habington married Richard Barneby, in whose family it remained for the next 400 years, although periodically (and confusingly) they changed their name to Lutley and back again to Barneby to maintain the inheritance.

THE NEW HOUSE

Richard Barneby added a two-storey stone extension to the east range about 1700, but otherwise few major changes were made until 1731, when Bartholomew Barneby inherited the estate. In 1737 he commissioned a new survey of the estate from John Perkins, but it was not until 1765 that he got the Shrewsbury architect Thomas Farnolls Pritchard (best known for the Iron Bridge at Coalbrookdale) to design him a new house. The building – a plain red-brick box – was less successful than its setting, in the midst of sweeping parkland with superb views over the Vale of Worcester to the east. (The house, which has lost its historic contents, is let and is not open to visitors.)

Above Gamekeeper William Dennett around 1909, when Lower Brockhampton was used as a shooting lodge

Below Mid-18th-century Brockhampton House (not open to visitors) was placed to enjoy the best of the views

BENIGN NEGLECT

Lower Brockhampton House became a modest farmhouse once again, occupied by farm tenants, and was quietly forgotten. This benign neglect prevented damaging modernisation, and by the late 19th century such romantic fragments of Olde England had come back into fashion. In the late 1860s John Habington Lutley consulted the antiquarian, architect and topographical draftsman J.C. Buckler, who supervised a thoroughgoing restoration of Lower Brockhampton.

Succeeding generations of Lutleys were conservative-minded countrymen who had neither the desire nor the means to make changes, so that by the time the last of the line, Colonel John Talbot Lutley, bequeathed Brockhampton to the National Trust in 1946, the estate was a rare and picturesque survival of a vanished age.

Below

The landscape gardener Thomas Leggett's grand 1769 scheme for remodelling the park

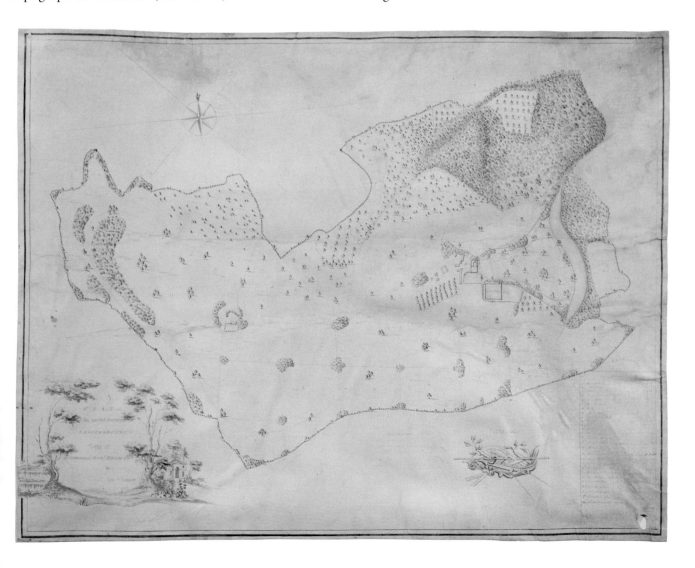

LOWER BROCKHAMPTON HOUSE

Lower Brockhampton is a rare survival of a medieval manorial complex, which may also once have included a village (long since disappeared).

THE EXTERIOR

Lower Brockhampton House is hidden away in a valley bottom, as its medieval builders valued access to water more highly than the views that excited the creators of the 18th-century Brockhampton House. It was built about 1380–1400 by John Domulton or his successor. The core of the house is the two-bay, south-facing Great Hall, to which the east service range is attached at right angles. The principal room in the east range was the Great Chamber on the first floor, which can be distinguished from the outside by the closely set vertical timbers. There may once have also been a matching west range at the other end of the Great Hall, traces of which were uncovered by the Herefordshire archaeology unit. J.C. Buckler's 1871 restoration was intended to return the house to its medieval form, but it entailed removing most of the doors and

Below The Great Hall fills the whole of the left-hand range. The Great Chamber occupied the first floor of the right-hand cross-wing

Restored with love
'The preservation of Brockhampton Old House has been a labour of love…. The attempt was regarded as hopeless except by its generous owners…. This is not ye only aged building, which, having been denounced as irreparable, has been rescued by the willing exertions of the writer.'
J.C. Buckler, 1871

windows, which may have been original. The National Trust made more modest repairs in the early 1950s and 1990s.

THE MOAT

The moat was originally larger, entirely surrounding the house. It was always more of a status symbol than a defensive feature, but it would at least have protected livestock herded inside it in unsettled times.

THE GATEHOUSE

This impossibly picturesque little building spans the moat somewhat tipsily. Like the moat, it was meant to charm and impress rather than exclude. Dendrochronology (tree-ring dating) dates it to about 1530–40. The delightfully decorative *bargeboards* carved with trailing vines are faithful reproductions of the decayed originals, but the studded *door* is a remarkable survival. The fabric was repaired in 1949–52 and again in 1999–2000.

THE CHAPEL

The chapel was probably built by the Brockhamptons around 1180. The octagonal *font* was carved from a single block of stone about the same date. The Domultons inserted the large *east window*, probably at the time they were building Lower Brockhampton House. The graveyard contains numerous burials – perhaps the remains of the inhabitants of the lost village. The *gravestones* that are still legible commemorate Richard Barneby (d.1719) and his wife Isabella (d.1726). The chapel had been abandoned by 1799, when John Barneby built a new estate church by the drive to his father's new house. The old chapel was swallowed up by the adjacent farmyard, being relegated to the status of a barn.

THE FARMYARD

The sounds and pungent smells of the nearby farm remind us that this remains a place of work as well as leisure. However, part of the farmyard and outbuildings have recently been adapted to provide room for families, school groups and a shop and to tell visitors more about Brockhampton and its history.

Below The half-timbered gatehouse was built about 1530-40 to create an unforgettable first impression of Lower Brockhampton

THE INTERIOR

THE SCREENS PASSAGE
This corridor divides the Great Hall (on the left) from the service rooms (on the right) – a typical medieval arrangement. Still *in situ* on the right-hand wall are two of the three original *doorheads* that would have led to the buttery, pantry and kitchen. The kitchen was moved to the stone extension when that was added to the east range about 1700.

THE GREAT HALL
The Great Hall was the largest and most important living space in any medieval house – the social heart of the entire household. It would originally have been very smoky, as it was heated by an open hearth in the centre of the room, and the smoke had to escape through an opening in the roof. The *fireplace* with its brick chimney was installed in the 17th century.

The grandeur of the Great Hall derives from the massive timbers from which it was constructed. They were felled on the Brockhampton estate and sawn to form '*base crucks*' – a type of construction reserved for the upper gentry. As their name suggests, base crucks rise vertically from floor level, but are jointed into a horizontal cross-piece (collar beam) to create a wider and more impressive space.

Before the age of powered cranes, raising such a framework was a considerable achievement. It is not surprising therefore that its creators left their handiwork exposed to be admired by all and decorated it with little battlements. The base crucks also served to divide up the space socially: the far bay was reserved for the owner and his family, who would have sat down to table on a raised dais.

Ground floor

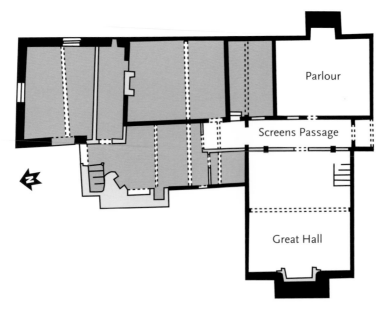

Parlour

Screens Passage

Great Hall

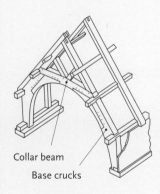

Collar beam

Base crucks

Left The Great Hall. The family would have sat on a raised dais (where the fireplace is now). The tables are a later addition

THE GREAT HALL

Pictures

The *portraits* are of 17th- and early 18th-century members of the Barneby family. They include Bartholomew Richard Lutley (1717–83), who changed his name to Barneby after he had inherited the estate and commissioned the new house from T.F. Pritchard.

Furniture

The three rare *refectory tables* would have been used by servants in 18th-century Brockhampton House. They are made of walnut with oak frames. The *court cupboard* is Welsh, *c.*1620. The *rush-light holders* were bought for the house at a local auction in 2001.

Hatchment

The *lozenge-shaped panel* over the fireplace commemorates Thomas Habington of Hindlip (d.1647), whose cousins had owned Brockhampton in the early 16th century. It also incorporates the coats of arms of the Brockhampton and Domulton families.

Weapons

Over the fireplace hang late 18th- and 19th-century sporting and military *guns* on racks more usually reserved for roasting spits. Guns were displayed here alongside African hunting spears in the late 19th and early 20th centuries, when Lower Brockhampton was used as a sporting lodge. Constance Sitwell was a guest at one such shooting party (see opposite).

Right The decoratively carved court cupboard may have been made in Wales

Above Muskets and rifles are hung over the fireplace on racks more normally used for roasting spits

A shooting party at Lower Brockhampton in autumn 1919

'The dining hall remained miraculously preserved, with its vaulted ceiling and uneven rafters; a long narrow table stood in the middle of it; and at the far end branches, heaped in the open hearth, and blazing, partly lit the dim place. A gallery, all made of oak cut from the place, ran round at the other end, with stairs, which sloped now, leading up to it. We busied ourselves unpacking the luncheon, laying the table, and setting out the drinks.'

Constance Sitwell

THE PARLOUR

This was originally part of the service quarters. In the late 17th century Thomas Barneby or his son John converted it into a comfortable panelled parlour. As so often in old houses, the panelling has been moved around.

THE GALLERY

The minstrels' gallery is all that is left of the first floor that was inserted into the Great Hall in the 17th century. Buckler probably inserted the balustrade as part of his 1871 restoration. The leather *fire buckets* were supplied by the company that insured Brockhampton House in the 19th century. The initials 'IB' stand for John Barneby (d.1817).

THE BEDROOM

The room is furnished with a 17th-century four-poster *bed* on loan from Caroline Compton of Croft Castle. The curtains, valance and bedspread are 1970s reproductions of 15th–16th-century crewelwork.

Opposite The Lutley Room
Below The Bedroom

THE LUTLEY ROOM

The room is dedicated to Colonel John Talbot Lutley, who gave Brockhampton to the National Trust in 1946, and is shown as a study. The pastel *portrait* of the Colonel was painted by Brian Hatton in 1915. The 18th-century *bureau* is said to have belonged to the 19th-century critic John Ruskin, who loved the traditional craftsmanship that ancient houses like Lower Brockhampton represented. Above the bureau are two decoratively illuminated *tenants' addresses* celebrating the Colonel's coming of age in 1894 and his safe return from the Boer War in 1901. The *survey* of the Brockhampton estate hanging above the chest was made by John Perkins in 1737.

Colonel Lutley

'A tall, ungainly, pipe-smoking countryman. Like many old bachelors of his generation he was shy, remote and rather gruff, albeit irreproachably polite.'

James Lees-Milne

FARMS, FARMERS AND FARMING: PAST

Farming may have undergone a mechanical revolution in the three centuries since John Perkins made his survey of the Brockhampton estate in 1737, but the crops grown (wheat, barley and grass) and the livestock raised (cattle, sheep and pigs) have changed surprisingly little.

Above The oast houses. What we eat and drink has always shaped the way we farm

Brewing at Brockhampton

One crop that has disappeared is hops, an essential ingredient of beer, which would have been brewed on the estate. Beer was a staple drink in the days before reliable clean drinking water was available. At Lower Norton Farm, you can still see two of the oast houses (with their characteristic conical roofs), in which the hops would have been dried. Although the oast houses are no longer in use, beer is once again being made at Brockhampton.

Land use by %	1737	2007
Arable (wheat and barley)	27.7	18.2
Hops	2.4	0
Orchard	2.4	5
Pasture	21.7	47.1
Meadow	6.3	0
Woodland	15.4	24.7
Coppice	7.3	1
Not specified	16.4	4

Foot-and-mouth disease

Livestock farming at Brockhampton was devastated by the outbreak of foot-and-mouth disease in spring 2000. The disease affects cloven-hoofed animals, especially cattle, sheep, pigs and deer, and while rarely fatal, makes them unsaleable. To stop the spread of the disease, almost all the stock on the estate had to be slaughtered, and access was severely restricted. The outbreak was eventually brought under control, but the cost for farmers and the tourist industry was very high. The National Trust did all it could to support affected farm tenants, including waiving their rent for a year.

Left John Perkins's 1737 survey of the Brockhampton estate

Right Foot-and-mouth disease closed much of the countryside to visitors

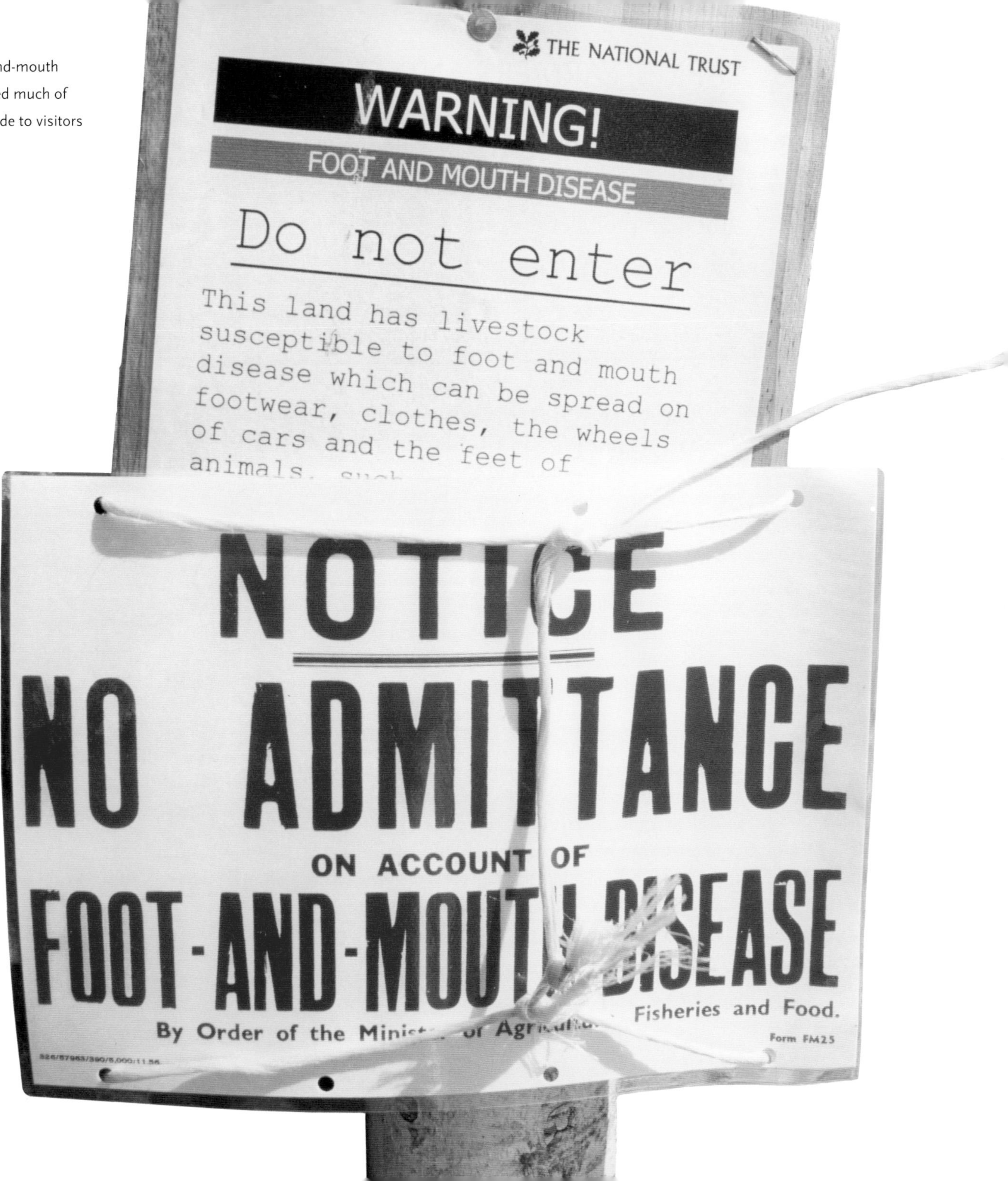

🍂 THE NATIONAL TRUST

WARNING!
FOOT AND MOUTH DISEASE

Do not enter

This land has livestock susceptible to foot and mouth disease which can be spread on footwear, clothes, the wheels of cars and the feet of animals, such

NOTICE
NO ADMITTANCE
ON ACCOUNT OF
FOOT-AND-MOUTH DISEASE

By Order of the Ministry for Agriculture, Fisheries and Food.

826/57953/390/5,000/11.56

Form FM25

FARMS, FARMERS AND FARMING: PRESENT

Ryeland sheep can be seen grazing the grass beneath the fruit trees in the Brockhampton orchards. The breed originated in Herefordshire, and the Brockhampton flock is one of the oldest in Britain, bred for its meat and short, but soft wool.

Above Tenant farmer James Hawkins in a maize field at Warren Farm

Below Ryeland sheep

Looking after the land

The Brockhampton farms were run on environmentally friendly lines long before the word 'environment' had become fashionable. This has been recognised by DEFRA (Department for Farming and Rural Affairs), whose Countryside Stewardship Scheme covers two farms on the estate. The scheme encourages farmers to restore traditional permanent pastures, replant and maintain hedgerows, and leave field margins uncultivated. Among the many benefits of returning to these traditional methods is a greater diversity of flora and fauna.

Welcoming visitors

Old ways sit happily alongside new ideas. Today's farmers know how to look after people as well as animals. The Oast House has been converted into holiday accommodation, and there are also four other holiday cottages on the estate. Warren Farm also provides teas and tours of the farm.

Right Hereford cattle feeding

Opposite

Top Oast House holiday cottage at Lower Norton Farm

Bottom Harvest time

Fighting back, farming forward

In 2002 Brockhampton was chosen as one of four pilot projects in the National Trust's Farming Forward in Action campaign, which seeks to manage its farms sustainably in partnership with its tenants, and support local people and businesses as they recover from the trauma of foot-and-mouth disease. Hereford cattle have been reared at Brockhampton since 1897. In 2003 the Brockhampton herds were restocked and they are once again being reared on natural grassland using old-fashioned, low-intensity methods. The top-quality meat that results is being marketed under a distinctive Brockhampton brand.

ORCHARDS

Fruit trees are often relatively short-lived, but at Brockhampton they have survived in hedgerows and fields thanks to the careful stewardship of its owners and tenant farmers over many years. The National Trust is keen to continue that tradition, and has restocked the 100 acres (40.5 hectares) of orchards with traditional local varieties of damson, apple, cherry plum and pear with the aid of donations and a grant from Covent Garden Soups. It has also reintroduced hives to the orchards that have a double purpose. The bees help pollinate the fruit and produce delicious honey which is sold in the farm shop.

The orchards are at their prettiest in spring, but come again in autumn and you will see the branches laden with fruit and decorated with the white berries of mistletoe, which grows profusely in Herefordshire. In 2000 the Trust's biological survey team identified the Mistletoe Weevil (*Ixapion variegatum*) in the Brockhampton orchards for the first time in Britain. This harmless creature, which measures only three mm long, is probably an overlooked native rather than a recent arrival.

Damson delights

Damsons were traditionally used to produce a rich red dye for the Cotswold cloth industry. Today, 'Shropshire prune' damsons are grown in the orchards around Lower Brockhampton House. Harvested by hand, the best fruit is selected to make a rich, tangy jam following an old family recipe handed down to the late Jane Coldicott. Damson jam made on the estate is on sale in the Brockhampton shop.

Above The white berries of mistletoe are a common sight in autumn

Below Picking damsons at Lower Brockhampton

Below Brockhampton damson preserve is made from fruit grown on the estate

The Brockhampton orchards in spring

'Have you ever been here when the blossom is out? ... It's heartbreakingly lovely, – the white blossom and the blue blue country stretching away beyond; there are damsons in the hedges, and cherries, and, most beautiful of all, the high old pear trees with their branches curling downwards.'

Constance Sitwell

Above Damsons have been growing in the Brockhampton hedgerows for centuries

WOODLAND

For anyone who loves trees, Brockhampton has much to offer: examples ancient and modern, large and small, ornamental and commercial, individual and *en masse*, youthful and decrepit. No fewer than 32 different species of tree have been recorded on the estate.

Broad-leaved trees

Brockhampton's historic woodland is chiefly made up of oak, ash, beech and sycamore trees, mixed with limes and sweet and horse chestnuts. Today, the mature oaks, some of which are over 500 years old, are admired for their gnarled beauty, but in past centuries, when houses and warships were largely constructed from wood, they provided an important cash crop and national strategic resource. Nowadays, nets are spread beneath their branches in autumn to collect acorns, which are planted at local nurseries to produce oaks for the future.

Right A Brockhampton beech in autumn

Below Charcoal burning

Conifers

The ancient woodlands are complemented by more recently introduced conifers. After the park was created in the mid-18th century, it was ornamented with redwood, cedar and pine, planted singly or in small clumps and also scattered across the permanent pasture. In the 1950s commercial plantations of Norway spruce, larch and Douglas fir were introduced to supply the local markets for Christmas trees and fence poles.

A woodland fuel

Woodlanders have been making charcoal for thousands of years, and in ancient woods the sites of their kilns can still be recognised by circles of blackened earth. The National Trust has revived this declining craft, slowly burning low-grade timber coppiced from the Brockhampton woodlands to produce a valuable and environmentally friendly end-product.

Life in death

In the past, fallen trees and branches were tidied away as unsightly. But since the Great Storm of 1987, it has increasingly been recognised that 'dead' wood actually teems with life, supporting valuable populations of insects, fungi and lichens. So don't be surprised to come upon decaying timbers that look as though they have been forgotten. The best policy is often to leave well alone.

Above Dead trees are often left to decay rather than removed, because they play host to numerous fungi and lichens

A forester remembers

'I do feel that Brockhampton has something special. There are a wide variety of trees that grow well on the clay soil, deep dingles, landscape views that you can never tire of seeing. An abundance of wildlife, badgers, foxes and all these living safely and freely, in some places where not even the forester has to do much other than check on the inhabitants.'

Les Rogers, Brockhampton property manager

WILDLIFE

Birds

Brockhampton's diverse habitats attract a wide range of different species throughout the year. In the deciduous woodlands, you are more likely to hear the distinctive hammering of lesser and greater spotted woodpeckers than to see them. Other woodland birds include pied flycatchers, redstarts and great tits. The conifer plantations draw jays and chiff-chaffs in spring to feed on pinecones. Hovering above clearings in the trees you may see buzzards, sparrowhawks and kestrels hunting for small mammals and other prey.

Bulfinchs are now a relatively uncommon sight in the springtime orchards, but their arrival is a mixed blessing at best, as they can strip a fruit tree of its buds in hours. Winter brings redwings and fieldfares.

Bats

Pippistrelle and long-eared bats roost in the outbuildings, along with the rarer lesser horseshoe bat. At dusk, they take to the air, swooping and circling over the parkland and lakes for insects, for which they compete with house martins and swallows.

Left Greater spotted woodpecker

Opposite

Top Common buzzard

Bottom Long-eared bat

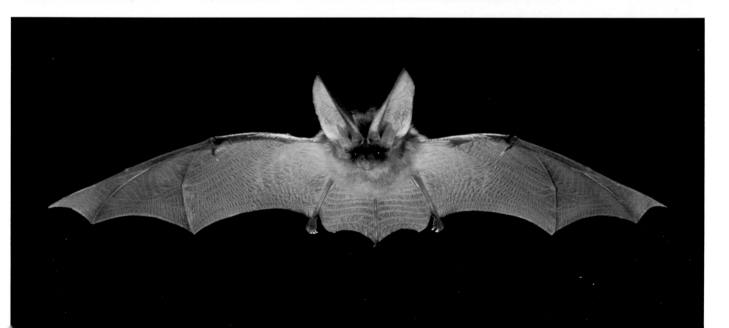

FLORA

In early spring, before the leaf canopy cuts out the light, the broad-leaved woods are awash with bluebells, snowdrops, daffodils and primroses. In early May, look out for sweet woodruff (*Galium odoratum*), which shoots out pretty little white flowers from six- or seven-leaved 'ruffs' – hence its name. Other native woodland plants include the wood spurge, with its yellowish-green flowers, and dog's mercury, another member of the spurge family that carpets woodland floors. As the name suggests, yellow archangel produces glowing yellow flowers, and is often to be found growing among bluebells, which are going over as it comes into flower in May. Less easy to spot is enchanter's nightshade, a member of the willowherb family which prefers dank secluded hedgerows and banks. It is supposed to have been the plant with which the sorceress Circe bewitched the crew of the Greek hero Ulysses in classical myth.

The older oak trees play host to numerous rare lichens. They may be less immediately appealing to the eye than the wild flowers on the woodland floor, but they are an encouraging indication that the air is clean and the habitat ancient and undisturbed.

Left Sweet woodruff
Middle Yellow archangel
Right Wood spurge